June 2014

TRAFFIC SAFETY

Alcohol Ignition Interlocks Are Effective While Installed; Less Is Known about How to Increase Installation Rates

GAO-14-559

TRAFFIC SAFETY

Alcohol Ignition Interlocks Are Effective While Installed; Less Is Known about How to Increase Installation Rates

Highlights of GAO-14-559, a report to the Chairman, Committee on Commerce, Science, and Transportation, U.S. Senate

Why GAO Did This Study

Motor vehicle crashes involving alcohol-impaired drivers killed 10,322 people in 2012 and account for almost one third of all traffic fatalities annually. Ignition interlocks are one strategy states use to combat DWI. In 2012, MAP-21 established a grant program for states that adopt and implement mandatory alcohol ignition-interlock laws for all convicted DWI offenders. Funding authorization for this program expires at the end of fiscal year 2014.

GAO was asked to review the effectiveness of ignition interlocks and NHTSA's implementation of the new grant program. This report discusses (1) what is known about ignition interlock effectiveness and (2) the extent to which NHTSA has assisted states in implementing ignition-interlock programs, including the grant program. GAO reviewed 25 studies that analyzed relationships between ignition interlocks and DWI arrests and fatalities; interviewed NHTSA officials and reviewed reports about NHTSA's assistance to states; and interviewed representatives from safety-advocacy and research organizations, and officials involved with ignition-interlock programs from 10 states. The states were selected based on grant program qualification and the number of alcohol-impaired fatalities, among other factors. The information from these states is not generalizable. DOT officials reviewed a draft of this report and generally agreed with the findings. DOT offered technical corrections, which we incorporated as appropriate.

View GAO-14-559. For more information, contact Susan Fleming at (202) 512-2834 or flemings@gao.gov

What GAO Found

Research GAO reviewed consistently indicated that when installed ignition "interlocks"—devices that prevent drivers from starting their cars if they have been drinking alcohol—effectively reduce the rate of re-arrest for driving while intoxicated (DWI) when installed. But once the devices are removed, DWI re-arrest rates return to pre-interlock rates. (Most studies use DWI arrest as a proxy for alcohol-impaired driving.) Further, the National Highway Traffic Safety Administration (NHTSA) estimated that between 15 and 20 percent of offenders arrested for DWI actually install ignition interlocks. Many factors contribute to low installation rates. For example, some states lack the resources to monitor offenders to ensure they install ignition interlocks; other states require that offenders pay fees and penalties to be eligible to install ignition interlocks and return to driving with interlocks. State ignition interlock programs vary in terms of how they are designed, but little research exists on which specific interlock program characteristics—such as monitoring or length of installation—could improve the effectiveness of interlock programs. NHTSA is currently conducting studies on factors that could help states improve installation rates or otherwise improve the effectiveness of their interlock programs. NHTSA expects these studies to be completed by 2015.

NHTSA has offered a variety of technical assistance, research, and education to help states establish and improve their ignition-interlock programs, as well as implement the ignition interlock grant program established by the Moving Ahead for Progress in the 21st Century Act (MAP-21). While state officials confirmed that NHTSA's overall ignition-interlock-related activities have been useful, some questioned NHTSA's implementation of the ignition interlock grant program. Specifically, NHTSA's implementation was based on the plain meaning of the authorizing language in MAP-21, which did not include any reference to exemptions. As a result, states with "employer exemptions"—programs that require offenders to drive only vehicles equipped with ignition interlocks for personal use but allow them to drive employer-owned vehicles for work purposes—were disqualified. Some state officials told us these exemptions are seldom used in practice, but are important to maintain because they facilitate the ability of offenders to work. According to NHTSA officials, they recognized that to qualify for the grant, many states would have to modify their ignition-interlock laws to make them applicable to first time offenders and eliminate exemptions; therefore, few states were expected to qualify in the grant's first years because it would be difficult for state legislatures to change their ignition-interlock laws in that time frame. In fiscal year 2013, 2 states qualified for the grant; most of the additional 12 states that applied for the grant were disqualified at least in part due to employer exemptions, but the legislatures in 2 of those states later removed such exemptions from their laws, resulting in 4 states qualifying for the grant in fiscal year 2014. Because the ignition interlock grant is relatively new, the extent to which additional state legislatures may be willing or able to modify their laws to qualify for the grant is unclear. A 2012 NHTSA review of states' impaired-driving laws found that at least 5 states' ignition-interlock laws included employer vehicle exemptions, but additional states had other factors that would prevent them from qualifying for the ignition-interlock grant.

Contents

Abbreviations

AIIPA	Association of Ignition Interlock Program Administrators
BAC	blood alcohol concentration
CDC	Centers for Disease Control and Prevention
DOT	Department of Transportation
DWI	driving while intoxicated
g/dL	grams per deciliter
GHSA	Governors Highway Safety Association
MADD	Mothers Against Drunk Driving
MAP-21	Moving Ahead for Progress in the 21st Century Act
NHTSA	National Highway Traffic Safety Administration
PRG	Preusser Research Group
TIRF	Traffic Injury Research Foundation

June 20, 2014

The Honorable John D. Rockefeller IV
Chairman
Committee on Commerce, Science, and Transportation
United States Senate

Dear Mr. Chairman:

In 2012, motor vehicle crashes involving alcohol-impaired drivers killed 10,322 people. While the number of such fatalities has dropped by 21 percent over the last 10 years, almost one third of all traffic fatalities annually resulted from crashes involving an alcohol-impaired driver over the same period. Breath alcohol "ignition interlocks" are devices that prevent a driver from starting a car if the device detects a driver's blood alcohol concentration (BAC) above a certain threshold.[1] Ignition interlocks represent one of the strategies states use to combat alcohol-impaired driving. California first piloted the use of ignition interlocks in 1986 for drivers convicted of driving while intoxicated (DWI).[2] According to the National Highway Traffic Safety Administration (NHTSA), all states have enacted legislation requiring or permitting the use of ignition interlocks. Historically, Congress has provided funds for state programs to reduce alcohol-impaired driving. Most recently, the 2012 surface transportation reauthorization act—Moving Ahead for Progress in the 21st Century Act (MAP-21)—also included funding for a new grant program for states with laws mandating that all drivers convicted of DWI be allowed to drive only vehicles equipped with an ignition interlock.[3] NHTSA assists states in implementing these programs and, in addition to other safety organizations, has funded research examining the effectiveness of ignition-interlock programs.

---

[1] BAC is measured as a mass of alcohol per volume of blood. In the United States, the standard measurement is represented as grams per deciliter (g/dL).

[2] The specific criminal offenses pertaining to alcohol-impaired driving vary across jurisdictions and can include such terms as "driving under the influence of alcohol or drugs (DUI)," "operating under the influence of alcohol or drugs (OUI)," or "driving while intoxicated (DWI)" In this report, the term "driving while intoxicated (DWI)" is used to capture all types of alcohol-impaired offenses.

[3] Pub. L. No. 112-141, 126 Stat. 405 (2012).

In light of the toll alcohol-impaired driving takes, you asked us to review the effectiveness of ignition interlocks and NHTSA's implementation of the MAP-21 ignition-interlock program. This report discusses (1) what is known about the effectiveness of ignition interlocks in reducing alcohol-impaired driving and (2) the extent to which NHTSA has assisted states in implementing ignition-interlock programs, including the MAP-21 ignition-interlock grant program.

To identify what is known about the effectiveness of ignition interlocks, we reviewed 25 studies conducted between 1990 and 2013 that analyzed relationships between ignition interlock devices or programs and alcohol-impaired driving outcomes, including DWI arrests and DWI fatalities. We identified these studies from a literature search and recommendations from organizations that conduct research on ignition interlocks, such as the Pacific Institute for Research and Evaluation. To identify the types of assistance that NHTSA provides to states to help them establish and implement their ignition-interlock programs, we interviewed NHTSA officials about their activities and reviewed reports describing NHTSA's ignition-interlock-related research, technical assistance, and conferences. For both objectives, we interviewed representatives from safety advocacy organizations such as the Governors Highway Safety Association (GHSA) and Mothers Against Drunk Driving (MADD). We also interviewed traffic safety, criminal justice, department of motor vehicles or licensing, and law enforcement officials from 10 states. The states were selected based on MAP-21 ignition-interlock grant program qualification, DWI fatality numbers in 2012 (most recent data available), and alcohol-impaired fatalities per 100-million vehicle-miles traveled as calculated by NHTSA. (See app. I for more information on scope and methodology and app. II for a list of reviewed studies.)

We conducted this performance audit from July 2013 to June 2014 in accordance with generally accepted government auditing standards, Those standards require that we plan and perform the audit to obtain sufficient, appropriate evidence to provide a reasonable basis for our findings and conclusions based on our audit objectives. We believe that the evidence obtained provides a reasonable basis for our findings and conclusions based on our audit objectives.

Background

While alcohol-impaired driving fatalities have declined from over 21,113 in 1982 to 10,322 in 2012, the proportion of such fatalities as a percent of total traffic-related fatalities has remained relatively constant—between 30 and 32 percent—over the past 15 years. Congress has targeted this persistent problem through legislation to encourage states to reduce their illegal per se BAC limit.[4] For example, beginning in 1982, federal legislation authorized grants to states to establish an illegal per se BAC limit of 0.10 or greater while driving a motor vehicle.[5] In other words, with respect to a BAC limit of 0.10, anyone whose blood contains 1/10th of 1 percent of alcohol or higher would be deemed to be DWI. In the late 1990s, Congress made grant funds available to states to encourage them to further lower the illegal per se driving BAC limit to 0.08. In 2000, the U.S. Department of Transportation Appropriations Act for fiscal year 2001 included a provision that states must enact 0.08 BAC laws by fiscal year 2004 or begin losing federal highway construction funds. According to NHTSA, all states had complied with that provision by 2004.

NHTSA administers safety-incentive grant programs to assist states in their efforts to reduce traffic-related fatalities, including alcohol-impaired fatalities.[6] NHTSA also provides guidance and technical assistance, sets and enforces safety performance standards for motor vehicles and motor vehicle equipment, and conducts research on driver behavior and traffic safety. As part of such research, NHTSA works with traffic safety organizations, such as GHSA, MADD, and the Traffic Injury Research Foundation (TIRF).

Through transportation legislation—including the Transportation Equity Act for the 21st Century[7], the Safe, Accountable, Flexible, Efficient Transportation Equity Act: A Legacy for Users[8], and MAP-21—Congress has provided funds to states for programs to combat impaired driving (sometimes called "countermeasure programs"). These grant programs

---

[4]Per se BAC laws establish the BAC level at which it is illegal per se (in itself) for a driver to operate a vehicle, regardless of the driver's apparent condition or actions.

[5]Pub. L. No. 97-364, § 101 (a), 96 Stat. 1738 (1982). Other federal legislation has been enacted with the goal of keeping alcohol-impaired drivers off the road, including reduced federal funding to states if they did not raise the minimum legal drinking age to 21 and the encouragement of "zero-tolerance laws" that set illegal per se BAC levels at 0.02 or greater for drivers under age 21.

[6]In fiscal year 2014, NHTSA requested a total budget of $828 million and 653 full time equivalent employees . NHTSA personnel are located in Washington, D.C. and among 10 regional offices.

[7]Pub. L. No. 105-178, 112 Stat. 107 (1998).

[8]Pub.L. No. 109-59, 119 Stat. 1144 (2005).

are designed to encourage states to adopt and implement effective programs to reduce driving under the influence of alcohol, drugs or the combination of alcohol and drugs. Under the most recent countermeasure program, states qualify for federal funding based on their impaired driving fatality rate and application requirements vary based on whether a state has a low-, mid-, or high-range fatality rate.[9] In addition, MAP-21 created a new grant program with funds available to reward states that implement laws requiring ignition interlocks for all individuals convicted of alcohol-impaired driving. Specifically,

- *"The Secretary [of Transportation] shall make a separate grant under this subsection to each State that adopts and is enforcing a mandatory alcohol-ignition interlock law for all individuals convicted of driving under the influence of alcohol or of driving while intoxicated."*[10]

MAP-21 made up to 15 percent per fiscal year of the total amount of the impaired-driving countermeasures grant available for the new ignition-interlock grant—about $21 million out of $139 million in fiscal year 2013. Any ignition-interlock grant funds that are not awarded remain available for grants under the broader impaired driving countermeasures grant program. In fiscal year 2013, 14 states applied for the grant and 2 were awarded funding, while in fiscal year 2014, 12 states applied and 4 were awarded funding. (See table 1.) States that qualify for this grant can use the funds for any authorized traffic safety program, including state ignition-interlock programs, other impaired driving countermeasures, or even traffic safety activities not related to alcohol-impaired driving. States categorized as low-range have the most flexibility in how they may use grant funds, while mid-range and high-range states must first obtain approval from NHTSA for some activities and meet certain conditions before they can be reimbursed. MAP-21 funding will expire at the end of fiscal year 2014; Congress is considering reauthorizing funding for

---

[9]NHTSA categorizes states as low-, mid- or high-range based on the average impaired driving fatality rate. (Fatality rate is fatalities per 100-million vehicle-miles traveled.) It is calculated based on the number of fatalities in motor vehicle crashes in a state that involve a driver with a blood alcohol concentration of at least 0.08 percent for every 100 million VMT. These calculations are based on Fatality Analysis Reporting System data from the most recently reported 3 calendar years for a state which are averaged to determine the rate. MAP-21 specifies that low-range states are those with an average impaired driving fatality rate of 0.30 or lower; mid-range states are those with an average impaired driving fatality rate higher than 0.30 and lower than 0.60; and high-range states are those that have an average impaired driving fatality rate of 0.60 or higher.

[10]See Section 31105(a) of MAP-21, Pub. L. No. 112-141, 126 Stat. 405, 748 (2012).

surface transportation programs—including the ignition-interlock grant program—for fiscal year 2015 and beyond.

Table 1: States That Applied For and Were Awarded MAP-21 Ignition-Interlock Grants, Fiscal Years 2013 and 2014

States that applied for the ignition-interlock grant	Fiscal year 2013 applicants and grant awards	Fiscal year 2014 applicants and grant awards
Alaska	$0	$0
Arizona	$0	$346,639
Arkansas	$0	$0
Colorado	$0	$0
Connecticut	$199,576	$205,258
Illinois	$0	$0
Kansas	$0	$0
Kentucky	a	$0
Louisiana	$0	a
New Mexico	$179,271	$184,375
New York	$0	a
Oregon	$0	$0
Utah	$0	a
Virginia	$0	$0
Washington	$0	$416,356
Total	**$378,847**	**$1,152,628**

Source: NHTSA. | GAO-14-559

[a]State did not apply for ignition-interlock grant.

The first ignition interlock was developed in 1969, but early models relied on alcohol sensors that were inconsistent in accurately identifying BAC. In the early 1990s, ignition interlock manufacturers began producing more reliable and accurate fuel cell sensors, which is a technology currently in use.[11] In 1992, NHTSA published model technical specifications for ignition interlocks that describe how ignition interlocks should perform and how the device can be calibrated to meet the model specifications. NHTSA updated these specifications in 2013.

---

[11]According to a 2013 MADD report, there were about 12 ignition interlock manufacturers and vendors in the U.S.

Ignition interlocks currently in use have four basic elements:

1. A breath alcohol sensor in the vehicle that records the driver's BAC and sends the signal to not start the engine if the BAC registers higher than the predetermined limit (see fig. 1);[12]

2. A retest system;[13]

3. A tamper-proof system for mounting the part of the unit that prevents the engine from starting, which is typically required to be inspected every 30 to 60 days to prevent circumvention; and

4. A data-recording system that logs the BAC results (for the initial test and retests) each time the vehicle is turned on and off, the time period the vehicle was driven and mileage, and other data that may be used by state authorities to monitor the offender's behavior.

---

[12]According to NHTSA, states' requirements for maximum BAC thresholds vary, but generally they are set at 0.02 or 0.025.

[13]The ignition interlock requires the driver to submit breath samples at random times to ensure that the driver does not drink alcohol after the engine has been started. The driver is given several minutes to exit traffic and move to a safe location to take the test. If the breathe sample is not provided or the sample exceeds the set point, the device may warn the driver and activate an alarm (e.g., horn blowing, lights flashing) that will continue until the ignition is turned off or a breath sample that is within the acceptable limits is provided. For safety reasons, the interlock device cannot turn off the vehicle's ignition once it has been started.

Figure 1: A Driver Using an Ignition-Interlock Device

Source: National Highway Traffic Safety Administration. | GAO-14-559

According to NHTSA, currently all states have enacted legislation requiring or permitting the use of ignition interlocks and they generally follow the same overall installation and removal process, according to Association of Ignition Interlock Program Administrators (AIIPA). (See fig. 2.)

Figure 2: A Generalized Depiction of an Ignition-Interlock Program

> **Arrest**
> Offender is arrested for driving while impaired (DWI) or refuses to submit to a breathalyzer test.

> **Pretrial**
> Judge may order interlock as condition of pre-trial release and/or department of motor vehicles (DMV) may suspend license, but allow offender to apply for a restricted interlock license.

> **Conviction**
> If convicted of DWI (either first or repeat), the state's ignition interlock law could limit the offender to interlock-restricted driving for months or years.

> **Coordination among court, DMV, and Law Enforcement**
> Court sends DMV the conviction information or court order for an interlock and DMV suspends the license until the device is installed. Law Enforcement databases are updated to reflect whether an offender's vehicle is required to have an interlock. If caught driving without a required ignition interlock, offenders may have their interlock period extended or be subject to other sanctions.

> **Installation and interlock-restricted driving privileges**
> • The offender selects an interlock vendor from a state-approved list. Vendor installs the interlock and teaches the offender how to use the device.
> • The offender typically pays between $65 and $90/month plus an installation and removal charge. DMV may also coordinate payment to the vendor if the offender qualifies for a state's indigent fund.
> • Once the vendor or the offender provides proof of installation, DMV issues an interlock (restricted) license.

> **Interlock data transferred and monitored**
> During periodic visits from offender, vendor uploads data and inspects ignition interlock. Vendor transmits data to DMV, courts, or other state agency for review. Failed blows, lockouts, or tampering could extend the interlock period or lead to other sanctions.

> **Required ignition interlock ends**
> DMV fully reinstates license; Conviction remains on offender's driving record for a certain number of years and is used to determine if he or she is a repeat offender if arrested or convicted again for DWI.

> **Removal**
> Vendor removes interlock from offender's vehicle when interlock period is completed.

Source: GAO analysis based on information from selected states and NHTSA. | GAO-14-559

State ignition-interlock programs vary in a number of ways:

- Program design—Some states may incorporate the use of ignition interlocks pretrial[14], while other states may stipulate ignition interlocks only upon conviction (i.e., a state sanctions a "license suspension" and then limits the offender to "interlock-restricted driving").[15] Some states impose interlock-restricted driving on all convicted DWI offenders, while in other states this is only required of those with multiple or high BAC convicted offenders.[16] Further, according to NHTSA, most states require a "hard suspension" period in which an offender's driving privileges are denied for a certain period of time before he or she may be eligible for interlock-restricted driving. State laws and requirements may prescribe ignition interlock requirements anywhere from a few months to as long as 10 years or more, often with progressively longer ignition interlock requirements for DWI offenders who are repeat offenders. Some states also exempt some DWI offenders from the application of their state interlock requirements. For instance, some states allow employer exemptions, which allow offenders to drive employer-owned vehicles without an ignition interlock for work purposes. Other states allow exemptions for medical reasons, such as allowing offenders who do not have the breath capacity to blow a sample into an ignition interlock to not be subject to the ignition-interlock installation requirement while at the same time suspending their license.

---

[14]For example, Washington's Department of Licensing administratively suspends an offender's license after arrest but before a DWI conviction. The state provides a period of time for the driver to contest such a sanction as a means for providing due process. This license suspension is separate from a DWI conviction, per se, as it can occur before trial.

[15]States may suspend or revoke DWI offenders' driving privileges pre- or post-conviction for a period of time or offer the offender an option for partial license reinstatement upon certain conditions such as the offender's installing an interlock. In some states, an offender may elect not to seek a partial license reinstatement, which is commonly referred to as "wait out." For the purposes of this report, we refer to the suspension or revocation of a driver's license or loss of driving privileges as imposed by either the state licensing authority or a judicial authority as a "license suspension" and we refer to the partial reinstatement of a driver's license or court-ordered limitations on driving privileges as "interlock-restricted driving."

[16]In some states, DWI offenders may not be eligible for interlock-restricted driving privileges because of additional factors related to their DWI offense. For example, in Illinois, first time DWI offenders who have caused great bodily harm or death were not eligible for interlock-restricted driving privileges.

- Program delivery—Requirements for interlock-restricted driving can be delivered programmatically in three different ways: through the judiciary within the criminal justice system, administratively within the driver licensing system, or using a hybrid approach that incorporates both judicial and administrative elements. According to AIIPA, 20 states have judicial programs, 20 states have administrative interlock programs, and 10 states have hybrid programs. According to NHTSA, in judicially-delivered interlock programs, judges have discretion to order interlock-restricted driving and can threaten harsher sanctions (e.g., jail time) for non-compliance. In contrast, administratively-delivered interlock programs are more uniform in imposing requirements for interlock-restricted driving on DWI offenders and can extend interlock periods or withhold driver's licenses (i.e., legal driving privileges) to encourage compliance, but have fewer sanction options at their disposal. There is a growing trend toward more hybrid programs.
- Oversight agency—In some states there may be a designated central authority that oversees implementation of certain aspects of the state's ignition-interlock program, such as a state department of transportation or state law enforcement authority. This agency's role may consist (1) of issuing state performance specifications for ignition interlocks; (2) of certifying the manufacturers' equipment for use by testing the equipment directly or by accepting test results as conducted by third party laboratories; (3) of approving ignition interlock vendors for business in the state; (4) of inspecting service centers; (5) of managing data from vendors; and (6) of managing state funds to assist indigent offenders with ignition interlock costs, among other things.
- Program cost and funding sources—Program costs vary with the design of each ignition-interlock program.[17] For example, states choosing to monitor ignition interlock data on individual offender BAC tests and driving habits will incur greater costs than states that do not. Programs that mandate offender appearances before a court or administrative body for elevated BAC tests will incur greater costs than programs that let the immediate inability to drive serve as the offender's sanction for an elevated test. States have varying approaches to funding the delivery of ignition-interlock programs, generally using fees paid by DWI offenders. Some states allocate

---

[17]According to NHTSA, states typically require offenders to pay the fees associated with an ignition interlock, which in most states range between $65 and $90 per month, plus approximately $100 to $250 for each installation.

some portion of collected fees to create indigent funds available to help low-income DWI offenders with ignition-interlock costs.

Research Indicates Interlock Devices Are Effective While Installed, but Installation Rates Are Low and Research on Strategies to Increase Rates Is Limited

Research we reviewed consistently indicated that ignition interlocks reduce the rate of re-arrest for DWI while they are installed on the vehicle, but once removed, DWI re-arrest rates return to pre-interlock rates. In addition, the percentage of DWI offenders who actually install an interlock when ordered is estimated to be low. Several factors contribute to this low rate, including low enforcement and monitoring to ensure offender compliance and costly fees and penalties that DWI offenders have to pay before they are eligible for interlock-restricted driving privileges. Little research exists on which specific interlock program characteristics may improve installation rates or otherwise improve the effectiveness of ignition-interlock programs, but NHTSA's ongoing and planned research—expected to be completed between 2014 and 2015—may fill this gap.[18]

Ignition-Interlock Devices Reduce Re-arrest While Installed

Research consistently indicated that ignition interlocks are effective while installed. That is, installation of ignition interlock devices in DWI offenders' vehicles reduces re-arrests for DWI when compared to alternative sanctions such as license suspension. Most studies use DWI arrest as a proxy for alcohol-impaired driving; however researchers have noted that arrest for DWI is a rare event, with some estimating that less than 1 percent of alcohol-impaired drivers are detected.[19] A 2011 review of literature assessing the effectiveness of ignition interlocks identified 15 studies (12 in the U.S., 2 in Canada, and 1 on Sweden) that observed that ignition interlock installation reduced the risk of being re-arrested for DWI offenders, compared to DWI offenders not using ignition interlocks. The studies included in this review primarily evaluated programs directed at drivers with multiple DWI offenses or first-time offenders with high BAC

---

[18]For research studies we included in our review, see appendix II.

[19]NHTSA officials noted that studies they reviewed showed that less that 1 percent of drivers who test positive for alcohol (BAC > 0.01) are arrested, and that 2 percent of those drivers considered impaired at the time of the study were arrested.

at arrest (usually >0.15).[20] As noted by the authors, the majority of studies in this review and those that we separately identified did not randomly assign participants to the ignition interlock; therefore, a limitation of many of these studies remains the potential for selection bias, as individuals who agree to install an interlock may be inherently different from individuals who do not agree to do so.[21] However, we did identify two randomized controlled trials, both in Maryland and limited to offenders with two or more alcohol-related traffic violations, that also found that ignition interlocks are effective at reducing re-arrests. The first, published in 1999, found that being in the interlock program—including installing an ignition interlock—reduced a driver's risk of committing a violation in the first year of the program by approximately 64 percent.[22] In 2011, researchers published a study that replicated the 1999 study with a new group of repeat offenders and found that participation in the ignition-interlock program still reduced drivers' risk of re-arrest by 36 percent while the ignition interlock was installed.[23]

Research we identified on the effectiveness of ignition interlocks also indicates that once the devices are removed, DWI arrest rates return to

---

[20]Findings regarding the effectiveness of ignition interlocks for first time offenders are unclear, based on study limitations. For example, some studies that aimed to parse out effects for first time offenders found no significant effects, possibly due to small numbers of first time offenders in the study sample (Tippets & Voas, 1998; EMT Group, 1990; DeYoung, Tashima, & Masten, 2005). Other studies not in this literature review only had aggravated first time offenders in their sample (such as offenders with a BAC > 0.20) which limits the generalizability of these studies to the first time offender population as a whole (Roth et al 2007; Morse & Elliott 1992). NHTSA has an ongoing study, which it expects to publish in 2014, on the association between state laws requiring all offenders to install ignition interlocks and the number of ignition interlocks installed.

[21]Additional limitations related to the body of literature we reviewed include the lack of a national study on interlock effectiveness and a lengthy time period over which the studies were conducted (between 1990 and 2013). Further, without randomization, there may be some judicial bias in that judges may choose offenders with certain characteristics for the intervention group. Despite these limitations, our review of the literature did provide support for the effectiveness of ignition interlocks while installed.

[22]Individuals may still be arrested for DWI while they have an interlock installed in their vehicle, for instance if they remove the device, or if they are driving a vehicle that does not have an interlock installed in it.

[23]The authors of this study attributed the difference in reductions in risk of re-arrest between the first and second randomized controlled trials to monitoring and length of installation, which will be discussed further below.

pre-interlock rates.[24] For example, a study of drivers with two or three DWI offenses in New Mexico observed a reduction in re-arrest while the ignition interlocks were installed, but in a period following removal of the ignition interlock, there was no significant difference in DWI re-arrest rates between offenders who had installed the ignition interlock and those who had not. The literature review of 15 studies came to the same conclusion that, following removal of ignition interlocks, re-arrest rates reverted to levels similar to those for comparison groups.

Several Factors Contribute to Low Installation Rates

Although ignition interlocks have been shown to reduce arrest for alcohol-impaired driving while installed, researchers we interviewed estimated that only 10 percent or less of DWI offenders ordered to install an ignition interlock actually install one.[25] NHTSA officials reported that between 15 and 20 percent of offenders arrested for DWI install ignition interlocks. Estimates in individual states vary, with one study of DWI offenders in California reporting about a 20 percent installation rate among those ordered to install.[26] A recent evaluation completed for the Washington Traffic Safety Commission reported 56 percent of DWI offenders ordered to install an ignition interlock did so.

However, estimating installation rates is imprecise. Federal officials told us that it is difficult to accurately estimate installation rates because the underlying data is often inconsistently maintained within and across states. For example, NHTSA officials told us that in an ongoing study of state ignition-interlock programs, they were able to identify only eight states with sufficient data (e.g., the number of ignition interlocks ordered and the number of DWI offenders who actually installed the ignition interlocks) to estimate the program's installation rate. As such, instead of using the number of individuals ordered to install an ignition interlock, one research group we spoke to used more easily-identifiable data such as total population, total DWI arrests, or total DWI fatalities. The resulting

---

[24]One of the Maryland studies mentioned above showed decreases in re-arrest rates once the ignition interlocks were removed.

[25]NHTSA officials noted that they suspected that this estimate is based on gross-level figures and is less accurate than the higher estimates.

[26]In the California study, offenders ordered to install an ignition interlock may have included both those convicted of DWI and of lesser Driving-While-Suspended charges.

measure is referred to as an installation "in-use" rate—for instance, the number of ignition interlocks in-use as a percentage of total population.

According to state officials, limited follow up and monitoring for compliance and prerequisites for eligibility can hinder installation.

Limited follow-up and monitoring for offender compliance—According to the literature review cited above, monitoring DWI offenders requires substantial administrative resources. Officials from several states included in our study said they do not have sufficient resources to follow up with offenders to ensure ignition interlocks have been installed once they have been ordered by a court or sanctioned by a state department of motor vehicles. For example, state officials in Texas told us that courts (i.e., judges) are often overwhelmed and do not have the resources to follow up with offenders to ensure that an ignition interlock has been installed or to monitor the results gathered by the ignition interlock devices. According to New York officials, the caseloads of some probation officers who may supervise DWI offenders are also heavy, and some probation officers may not necessarily prioritize ignition interlock compliance. Other law enforcement entities, even those that may lead or operate the state's ignition-interlock program, may not have the resources to follow up on offenders to ensure ignition interlocks have been installed and used as required. For example, Washington's program is overseen by the state highway patrol, but according to a senior Washington official, the program lacks the resources to identify offenders who may be illegally driving with a suspended license (i.e., those offenders who claim to be waiting out the period of time that their license was suspended by not driving at all) or driving without an ignition interlock.

Moreover, state officials we interviewed stated that limited followup and monitoring contributed to offenders' decisions to wait out ignition interlock requirements. As mentioned above, the likelihood of being stopped for a traffic violation is estimated to be less than 1 percent of those driving while impaired by alcohol and research suggests that DWI offenders continue to drive while their licenses are suspended. Officials from New York described that a continuing challenge to increasing the number of installed interlocks were DWI offenders attempts to wait out the period an ignition interlock is required by temporarily signing over their vehicles to friends or family. According to these officials, in New York, quarterly inquiries are made to each of 62 counties' probation departments to check vehicle registrations of DWI offenders to address such attempts to circumvent the state's requirements for ignition interlocks. According to an Illinois official, there is no requirement that an offender install an ignition interlock in order to reinstate his or her license[27] and that requirements for interlock-restricted driving were undermined because many DWI offenders believed that they could avoid being caught while driving without an ignition interlock.

Prerequisites for eligibility—There are a variety of conditions a DWI offender may be required to satisfy before he or she can receive interlock-restricted driving privileges.

- Fees and penalties—In some states, offenders may have to pay fees and penalties before they can be eligible to install an ignition interlock and receive a restricted license. One study of Florida's ignition-interlock program found that half of DWI offenders who had completed their revocation period were still ineligible to install an ignition interlock because they had not paid required fines and tickets. Similarly, an Illinois official stated that a DWI offender would have to pay at least a $380 fee in addition to any outstanding fees or penalties and enter into a payment plan for any judgments resulting from the DWI conviction in order to be eligible for interlock-restricted driving privileges. Likewise, Connecticut requires offenders to pay a $100 fee before an ignition interlock is installed. These fees and penalties are in addition to any costs paid to the vendor for installation or lease of the interlocks. Even in some states where there are indigent funds available to assist offenders with the cost of ignition interlocks, some of these fees imposed by the state may not be waived or reduced.[28] In Texas, one official described how mandatory license surcharges have contributed to a substantial number of offenders driving illegally and without insurance.

---

[27]This contrasts with a state like Washington, where an offender must have an interlock installed and have a certain number of consecutive months without BAC tests registering above the predetermined level in order for their license to be reinstated.

[28]For example, in Washington, an offender seeking interlock-restricted driving privileges must pay $100 to apply for reinstatement. However, if he or she qualified for assistance from Washington's indigent fund, this assistance may only be used for vender fees (i.e., costs associated with ignition-interlock installation, lease, removal, and transfer to another vehicle) and not for the application fee. Furthermore, some states with indigent funds have experienced challenges with the demand for this assistance. Washington officials stated that the number of interlock drivers receiving support from the indigent fund grew from 3,066 in 2009 to 19,267 by December 2013, and the amount disbursed increased from $775,643 to more than $1.4 million between 2011 and 2013. Washington officials said that the number of applicants was beginning to exceed available funds.

- Treatment programs—In some states, offenders must complete treatment programs before they are eligible to install an interlock and have interlock-restricted driving privileges. In Illinois, offenders may be required by a hearing officer or judge to enter or complete treatment, in conjunction with installing an interlock, as conditions for being granted a restricted drivers license. Likewise, in New York, officials noted that some jurisdictions will not allow offenders to obtain their licenses until treatment has been completed.

Limited Research Exists on Which Program Characteristics Could Improve Installation or Overall Program Effectiveness

Research supports the effectiveness of ignition interlocks in combating impaired driving while they are installed, but limited research exists on how to improve installation rates.

Table 2: Summary of Ignition-Interlock Effectiveness Research

Effectiveness research topic	Substantial research[a]	Limited research[a]	Ongoing, unpublished studies
Interlock Devices			
Effective when installed	X		
Effect disappears when interlock is removed	X		
Interlock Programs			
Characteristics that could <u>increase installation</u>, such as: • harsher alternatives • requiring an interlock for license reinstatement		X	X[b] (NHTSA)
Characteristics that could <u>reduce re-arrest during and after</u> installation, such as: • length of installation • combining treatment with the interlock program • monitoring		X	X (NHTSA[b], CDC[c])

Source: GAO. | GAO-14-559

[a]We refer to research as "substantial" if we identified five or more articles published on the topic whose results we determined to be reliable. We refer to research as "limited" if we identified fewer than five articles published on the topic whose results we determined to be reliable.

[b]NHTSA has a cooperative agreement with GHSA, which contracted with the Preusser Research Group to evaluate state ignition interlock use and re-arrest rates in 28 states. NHTSA expects these studies to be published by 2015.

[c]The Centers for Disease Control and Prevention (CDC) is currently analyzing the effect of treatment on re-arrest. The CDC expects to publish this study in 2015 at the earliest.

Characteristics That Could Increase Installation: Harsher Alternatives, License Reinstatement

Two studies of programs in U.S. counties where judges required stricter penalties for those not installing an ordered ignition interlock found a higher percentage of offenders installed the ignition interlock. According to a 2001 study, a court in Hancock County, Indiana, had required installation of interlocks for all offenders using the threat of jail or electronically monitored house arrest for non-compliance since 1997. The study estimated that 62 percent of DWI offenders installed an ignition interlock.[29] A 2010 NHTSA evaluation of the New Mexico ignition-interlock program found that 71 percent of convicted DWI offenders installed an interlock in Santa Fe County, where judges made house arrest the alternative to ignition interlock installation. In cases where DWI offenders pleaded they had no vehicle, the judge required them to wear an electronic monitoring bracelet.[30] According to a 2013 MADD report based on workshops with state officials and stakeholders from more than 30 states, imposing harsher sanctions could be a strategy for increasing installation rates. One state official we interviewed described that mandating alcohol monitoring as an alternative to installing an interlock would be effective in increasing the installation rates.

One study suggested that requiring an ignition interlock for license reinstatement following a DWI could improve installation rates. As mentioned above, one of the ways a DWI offender can avoid installing an interlock is by simply waiting out the ordered suspension period and not driving during that time. Yet research suggests that many DWI offenders drive during a suspension period.[31] However, if a state has a separate

---

[29]This refers to the percentage of offenders who installed interlocks, not the additional percentage attributable to Hancock County's program; the authors did not measure the rates of interlock installation in the surrounding counties, so we cannot isolate the effect of Hancock County's stricter program. In addition, the 95 percent confidence interval for this installation rate extends from roughly 50 percent to 74 percent.

[30]An electronic monitoring bracelet is a device worn on an offender's ankle that electronically tracks his or her location. In order to enforce house arrest, the bracelet is linked by telephone lines to a main computer system that sends off a constant signal. If the offender strays beyond the court-authorized radius of the receiver, the computer system records the date and time that the interruption occurred. If the interruption occurred at a time when the offender was scheduled to be at home, a parole officer or other monitoring agent checks into the violation and additional sanctions may result.

[31]Ignition-interlock studies cited in this report often use license suspension as the control group. As stated above, ignition interlocks are more effective than license suspension, which means that many DWI offenders continue driving and being re-arrested while their licenses are suspended.

administrative requirement through the department of motor vehicles, for example, the offender cannot simply wait out the suspension period and will have to install an ignition interlock in order to reinstate his full license. A 2013 study on a Florida state requirement that DWI offenders install an ignition interlock for at least 6 months in order to fully reinstate their license observed that nearly 100 percent of offenders eligible to install an interlock actually did so.[32] According to state officials, New Mexico and Washington have a similar license reinstatement requirement.

NHTSA is currently working with the Preusser Research Group (PRG) to conduct a study on factors that could help states improve installation rates. This research is being supported jointly by NHTSA and the CDC, through a cooperative agreement with GHSA, which in turn contracted with PRG to examine state ignition-interlock program characteristics—such as state laws, penalties, monitoring, or other factors—that were associated with higher ignition interlock use. NHTSA officials said they expect this report to be issued by late summer 2014.

Characteristics That Could Reduce Re-arrest during and after Interlock: Monitoring, Length of Installation, and Treatment

A randomized controlled trial of DWI multiple offenders in Maryland observed that closer monitoring of offenders' breath tests into the interlock device improved compliance with the ignition-interlock program. Closer monitoring consisted of reviewing breath test data and sending letters to offenders informing them of the results and consequences. The control group was subject to the standard Motor Vehicle Administration monitoring, which did not include any specific procedures for monitoring offenders. For example, the Motor Vehicle Administration took no action when offenders in this group disconnected the interlock or logged numerous breath tests at or above the limit of the ignition interlock. The authors found that the closely monitored group had significantly fewer initial breath test failures when attempting to start their vehicles than the control group did. The authors also observed that ignition interlock disconnects (e.g., tampering with the device) and retest failures were lower for the closely monitored group as well, although these latter differences were not statistically significant. Through the GHSA study mentioned above, NHTSA officials told us that NHTSA and the CDC hope to identify state's ignition-interlock program characteristics, such as

---

[32]Many offenders were not eligible to install an interlock during the time of the study. In Florida, as noted above, offenders must complete outstanding sanctions (e.g., tickets, fines) before being eligible to install an ignition interlock.

monitoring, that may be associated with lower re-arrests. NHTSA officials said this study should be completed by 2015.

We identified one study on the impact of varying lengths of ignition-interlock installation on DWI re-arrest. The study compared the results of the Maryland's two randomized controlled trials mentioned above (2011 and 1999) in order to determine whether the later 2-year administrative ignition-interlock program was more effective in reducing recidivism than the earlier 1-year interlock program. The 2011 study did show a significant reduction in re-arrest even after the interlock was removed, a result that the authors attributed to the extension of the interlock period from 1 year to 2 years, although other differences in the two randomized controlled trials, such as increased monitoring, were noted as well.[33] Despite this research, authors of the literature review mentioned above noted that research currently provides little guidance on the ideal length of interlock program participation. Research and interviews we conducted suggests that most states require installation for at least 5 months.

According to researchers, pairing interlock use with alcohol treatment could be key to reducing re-arrest once the interlock is removed, but we did not find any published studies evaluating the combination of interlock use with treatment programs. Four studies in our review observed the drinking patterns of DWI offenders while they participated in an ignition-interlock program, and two of these suggested that this data could be used to target treatment to specific offenders.[34] This has led researchers and NHTSA officials to posit that treatment could reduce the overall amount of drinking and potentially have an effect even after the ignition interlock is removed. The CDC is currently conducting a study on the

---

[33]A 2014 Washington state report on its ignition-interlock program observed reductions in re-arrest for DWI during a 2-year period following ignition interlock installation, and hypothesized that this could have been due to longer installation periods, among other factors. The study observed differences in re-arrest rates for first, second, and third-plus DWI offender groups whose installation periods averaged 10.4, 13.3, and 13.8 months, respectively. However, the study was not designed to evaluate the impact of length of installation.

[34]Authors of two of these studies, conducted in Canada, noted that the BAC results cannot be matched directly to the offender, but believe this limitation is mitigated by findings from other studies that show that primarily the offenders are the ones driving the interlocked vehicles. Authors of the other two studies noted that the vendor data they used contained no demographic information and so they were not able to distinguish between types of offenders.

effect of a Florida state law that required alcohol treatment for DWI offenders who fail a certain number of breath tests on their installed ignition interlocks. CDC officials told us the results of this study would be published in 2015 at the earliest.

NHTSA Provided Assistance to States for Ignition-Interlock Programs, but Some State Officials Questioned NHTSA's Implementation of MAP-21 Grant

NHTSA offered a variety of assistance—including guidance, technical assistance, research, and education—to help states establish and improve their ignition-interlock programs, including the new ignition-interlock grant established by MAP-21. State officials who administered ignition-interlock programs confirmed that NHTSA's activities were helpful. However, some officials questioned NHTSA's implementation of the ignition-interlock grant program because the states that exempted certain offenders from installing interlocks were disqualified. According to some state officials, exemptions are seldom used in practice, but are important to maintain because they facilitate the ability of offenders to work.

NHTSA Assisted States in Their Efforts to Implement Ignition-Interlock Programs

NHTSA offered a variety of assistance to help states establish and improve their ignition-interlock programs. Specifically, NHTSA developed and shared guidance, issued technical specifications, sponsored research studies, collaborated with industry experts, and funded technical assistance. It also administered and oversaw grants to states.

- **Guidance:** Since 2008, NHTSA has published reports highlighting key features of state ignition-interlock programs, including most recently the 2013 guideline for a model ignition-interlock program.[35] In general, these reports provide information about ignition-interlock program features and highlight issues that states should consider as they put together or further refine their ignition-interlock programs.
- **Technical Specifications:** In 1992, NHTSA published technical model specifications for ignition interlocks that describe how ignition interlock devices should perform and indicate how they can be calibrated to meet uniform standards. In May 2013, NHTSA revised the model specifications to address the rapid technological

---

[35]U.S. Department of Transportation, National Highway Traffic Safety Administration, *Model Guideline for State Ignition-interlock Programs*, Report Number DOT HS 811 859 (December 2013).

innovations in the industry that had occurred since the original publication. State ignition-interlock program administrators used these model specifications to certify interlock devices offered by manufacturers and ensure vendors and installers meet uniform performance standards.

- **Research:** NHTSA funds research studies that assess and provide a more scientific basis for assertions about the effectiveness of ignition interlock devices. Since 2009, NHTSA has funded and published a number of studies and reports on ignition interlocks, including the ongoing studies mentioned above on factors that could help states improve installation rates or program characteristics related to lower re-arrest rates.

- **Collaboration:** NHTSA, either directly or through grants to other organizations, brought stakeholders and experts together to share information and collaborate on specific ignition-interlock program projects. For example, in 2007, NHTSA funded an expert panel to gather views about the effectiveness of ignition interlocks in preventing impaired driving offenses; the views were published in a 2010 NHTSA report. In 2010, NHTSA and GHSA jointly hosted a national ignition interlock summit, extending invitations to state highway safety representatives and ignition-interlock program administrators from all 50 states, interlock manufacturers, researchers, and national organizations. NHTSA published a report summarizing the summit in 2011. NHTSA also signed a cooperative agreement with MADD for the organization to hold a series of ignition interlock institutes across the U.S. between August 2009 and October 2012. The institutes were designed to bring together teams of people and various agencies that are involved with some component of their state ignition-interlock program in order to identify program improvements.

- **Technical Assistance:** In 2007, NHTSA entered into the first of two cooperative agreements with TIRF to support the development of a curriculum about ignition-interlock programs and to provide direct assistance to states that seek to improve their ignition-interlock programs. At the request of a state's highway safety office, TIRF consultants review the state's ignition-interlock program, analyze the program's processes, and identify possible solutions for any weaknesses. For example, in 2009, TIRF examined Illinois' ignition-interlock program and identified a number of program strengths and challenges. TIRF recommended that the state develop a process for limiting the number of offenders who can opt out of the interlock program, among other things. NHTSA's cooperative agreement with TIRF to provide technical assistance ends in August 2017.

- **Grants Administration:** NHTSA also assisted state officials to apply for DOT safety grants, such as the impaired driving countermeasures grant, that can be used for their state's ignition-interlock program. For example, the agency held webinars and conducted other outreach to educate states about the requirements of the new ignition-interlock grant program.

State officials indicated that NHTSA's actions assisted them in implementing and further refining their ignition-interlock programs. For example, two state officials noted that by attending conferences sponsored by NHTSA they were able to leverage the experiences of other states whose programs were more mature. Others noted that NHTSA's regional staff were readily available to answer questions and provide advice and technical assistance. State officials also mentioned that they used NHTSA's ignition-interlock reports and guidance, such as the 2013 Model Guidelines report, to identify ways to strengthen their programs.

Some State Officials Questioned NHTSA's Implementation of the New Grant

State officials questioned how NHTSA implemented one aspect of the new ignition-interlock grant program; specifically that states did not qualify for funding if they included exemptions in their alcohol ignition-interlock programs. As described previously, states qualify for this grant by requiring that all individuals convicted of a DWI offense be limited to driving motor vehicles equipped with an ignition interlock. Under NHTSA's implementation regulations, states must require that the ignition interlock be used for a minimum period of 30 days. As implemented by NHTSA, states whose ignition-interlock programs allowed DWI offenders to drive vehicles without an ignition interlock for work and medical reasons did not qualify for the grants because their programs were not considered mandatory for all such convicted individuals. Officials from New York, Illinois, Washington, and Arizona indicated that NHTSA disqualified their state because of the employer vehicle exemptions to their state's ignition-interlock requirements. Illinois and New York officials stated that although their state's statutes allow exemptions, their programs typically grant few exemptions compared to the number of ignition interlocks installed, and the officials did not believe that exemptions substantially diminished the effectiveness of their ignition-interlock program. However, state officials noted they did not track the specific number of employer vehicle exemptions that have been granted. For example, in New York, employer vehicle exemptions are filed at the county level, not at the state level (i.e., with a state level department), and the state has little ability to access the data in order to estimate the number of employer vehicle exemptions that had been granted or compare this to the number of ignition interlocks ordered.

NHTSA officials stated that they based their implementation of the ignition-interlock grant on the plain meaning of the authorizing language in MAP-21, which did not include any reference to exemptions or exclusions.[36] In responding to our draft report, the Department of Transportation (DOT) provided a document that contained information on states' ignition-interlock laws.[37] Specifically, NHTSA's *Digest* indicated that as of May 2012 at least 5 states allowed exemptions for employer vehicles, and additional states had other factors that would prevent them from qualifying for the ignition-interlock grant. NHTSA officials noted that the MAP-21 grant represents a high bar for many states. Based on experience in reviewing state impaired driving laws, NHTSA officials recognized that many states would have to change existing laws to apply to first time offenders and eliminate exemptions. Few states were expected to qualify in the grant's first years because it would be difficult for state legislatures to change their ignition interlock laws in that time frame. Further, NHTSA officials noted that the agency did not receive comments from states related to exemptions during the public comment period for the interim final rule.[38]

Some state officials noted that it would be challenging to change their laws to qualify for the ignition-interlock grant. First, officials from several states told us that there is a lack of political support to put in place requirements for first time offenders or to eliminate exemptions. State officials from two states reported that their legislatures would not want to impede employment of offenders, particularly in a poor economic climate

---

[36]Statutory construction includes and often begins with construing the "plain meaning" of the statutory language itself to determine whether the language at issue has a plain and unambiguous meaning.

[37]DOT periodically compiles and publishes comprehensive information on state impaired-driving laws in its *Digest of Impaired Driving and Selected Beverage Control Laws*. DOT officials stated that they anticipate updating the publication in 2016 or 2017. See U.S. Department of Transportation, National Highway Traffic Safety Administration, *Digest of Impaired Driving and Selected Beverage Control Laws, 27th Edition*, Report Number DOT HS 811 796 (May 2012).

[38]NHTSA officials also noted that exemptions in any form can undermine the intended benefits of traffic safety laws and allowing offenders to drive without ignition interlocks through the use of exemptions could negatively impact traffic safety.

and given the expanse of areas in states that are rural, which makes driving a necessity for daily life. Some state officials also pointed out that the small size and short term nature of the grant funding did not support making changes to their states' ignition-interlock programs to qualify for the MAP-21 ignition-interlock grant program.

Despite these challenges, two state legislatures changed their laws to eliminate exemptions to qualify for the ignition-interlock grant in fiscal year 2014. During the first year of the grant—fiscal year 2013—only 2 states out of 14 that applied qualified for the grant. Most of the states that did not receive the grant were disqualified due to employer exemptions. State legislatures in Arizona and Washington[39] were able to eliminate employer exemptions and other disqualifying factors from their laws in order to qualify for the grant in fiscal year 2014, bringing the total grant recipients to four that year. Because the ignition-interlock grant is relatively new, the extent to which additional state legislatures would be willing or able to modify their laws to qualify for the grant is unclear.

Concluding Observations

Ignition interlocks are one promising tool states can use to combat alcohol-impaired driving. However, in order to be effective, the devices must first be installed in vehicles and several factors—including limited monitoring and eligibility prerequisites—can hinder installation even when DWI offenders are ordered to use ignition interlocks. Ongoing and planned research by NHTSA and others may shed light on actions state officials can take to increase installation rates and otherwise improve the effectiveness of their ignition-interlock programs. The MAP-21 ignition-interlock grant also has the potential to encourage the increased use of ignition interlocks by providing funds to states that require the use of an ignition interlock for all individuals convicted of a DWI offense. In the first 2 years of the grant program, few states applied for the grant and of those, most were disqualified because of exemptions that allowed DWI offenders to drive employer-owned vehicles without ignition interlocks. Following the first grant year, two state legislatures modified their state ignition-interlock laws to eliminate employer and other exemptions, thereby qualifying for the MAP-21 grant in 2014. The extent to which

---

[39]Washington changed its laws so that employer exemptions could not be used in the first 30 days after a convicted DWI first-time offender is limited to interlock-restricted driving. For repeat offenders, employer exemptions may not be used for the first 365 days of interlock-restricted driving.

other states may follow suit is unclear. Some state officials noted that even though these exemptions are not widely used, this option is critical to allow DWI offenders to retain their jobs, particularly in rural areas or areas without public transportation. For such states, the incentive and relatively limited funding offered by the grant is not likely to outweigh the challenges of changing state ignition-interlock laws to eliminate exemptions.

Agency Comments

We provided a draft of this report to DOT for review and comment. Included in the draft report was a recommendation that the Secretary of Transportation provide Congress with information about the extent to which states' ignition interlock laws allow exemptions. This recommendation was intended to provide Congress with more complete information as it considers reauthorizing surface transportation programs, including the ignition-interlock grant program. On June 11, 2014, the Deputy Director of Audit Relations transmitted DOT's comments by email. In responding to our draft report, DOT officials expressed concerns about this recommendation and provided additional information that addressed our recommendation. Specifically, DOT provided the *Digest of Impaired Driving and Selected Beverage Control Laws,* which is a compilation of comprehensive information on states' impaired-driving laws. We concluded that the *Digest* includes sufficient information to provide an overview of the extent to which state laws allow exemptions and addresses our proposed recommendation. Therefore, in light of the new information that DOT provided, we withdrew our recommendation. DOT also provided technical corrections, which we incorporated as appropriate.

As agreed with your office, unless you publicly announce the contents of this report earlier, we plan no further distribution until 30 days from the report date. At that time, we will send copies to the appropriate congressional committees, the Secretary of Transportation, and other interested parties. In addition, the report will be available at no charge on the GAO website at http://www.gao.gov.

If you or your staff have any questions about this report, please contact me at (202) 512-2834 or flemings@gao.gov. Contact points for our Offices of Congressional Relations and Public Affairs may be found on the last page of this report. GAO staff who made key contributions to this report are listed in appendix III.

Sincerely yours,

Susan A. Fleming
Director, Physical Infrastructure Issues

Appendix I: Objectives, Scope, and Methodology

The objectives of our review were to determine (1) what is known about the effectiveness of ignition interlocks in reducing alcohol-impaired driving and (2) the extent to which the National Highway Traffic Safety Administration (NHTSA) has assisted states in implementing ignition-interlock programs, including the Moving Ahead for Progress in the 21st Century Act (MAP-21) ignition-interlock grant program.

To identify what is known about the effectiveness of ignition-interlock programs, we conducted a literature search for studies that analyzed relationships between ignition interlock devices or programs and alcohol-impaired driving outcomes, including DWI arrest and DWI fatality. We started with a 2010 NHTSA report "*Key Features for Ignition Interlock Programs,*" which cited 15 studies and highlighted programs and program features that are believed to be best able to serve traffic safety interests, including reducing alcohol-impaired driving. We then identified additional existing studies from peer-reviewed journals, government reports, and conference papers based on searches of various databases, such as ProQuest, MEDLINE, and Transportation Research International Documentation. Search parameters included studies across the U.S. and in specific states and those on specific interlock program components, such as mandatory for first and repeat offenders and length of installation required. These parameters resulted in 280 abstracts, which we narrowed to 96, in part by cross-referencing the list with Web of Science, a resource that identifies highly cited articles. We also conducted interviews with organizations that conduct research on ignition interlocks, such as the Pacific Institute for Research and Evaluation, and asked them to recommend additional research.

From these multiple sources, we identified 25 peer-reviewed articles, government reports, and conference papers between 1990 and 2013 that were relevant to our research objective on the effectiveness of ignition interlocks in reducing alcohol-impaired driving. To assess the methodological quality of the selected studies, we performed an initial in-depth review of the findings, and then a GAO methodologist performed an independent assessment of the study's methodological soundness and confirmed our reported analysis of the finding. One limitation is that the majority of studies we identified did not randomly assign participants to the ignition interlock; therefore there remains the potential for selection bias, as individuals who agree to install an interlock may be inherently different from individuals who do not agree. Additional limitations related to the body of literature we reviewed include the lack of a national study on interlock effectiveness, a lengthy time period over which the studies were conducted (between 1990 and 2013), and the reliance of DWI arrest as a proxy for alcohol-impaired driving. Despite these limitations, our review of the literature did provide support for the effectiveness of ignition interlocks while installed.

We supplemented our synthesis by interviewing three of the studies' authors who had each contributed to multiple studies. We also conducted interviews with NHTSA officials, as NHTSA has contracted out some published and ongoing research on the effectiveness of ignition interlocks. We also discussed program effects with state ignition-interlock program administrators from the 10 states we included in our review (as discussed below) and with NHTSA officials who were knowledgeable about NHTSA-funded published and ongoing research on the effectiveness of ignition interlocks.

To identify the types of assistance that NHTSA provides to states to help them establish and implement their ignition-interlock programs, we interviewed NHTSA officials about their activities and reviewed reports describing NHTSA's ignition interlock-related research, technical assistance, and conferences. For both objectives, we interviewed representatives from safety advocacy organizations such as the Governors Highway Safety Association and Mothers Against Drunk Driving. We also interviewed traffic safety, criminal justice, department of motor vehicles or licensing, and law enforcement officials from a nongeneralizable sample of 10 states. The selected states—Arizona, Connecticut, Illinois, Montana, New Mexico, New York, Pennsylvania, South Carolina, Texas, and Washington—were chosen to reflect a mix of states that applied and did not apply for, as well as, states that qualified and were disqualified from the MAP-21 ignition-interlock grant program. To further select among states, we identified states with high DWI fatality numbers in 2012 (the most recent year for which data are available) and DWI fatality rates (alcohol-impaired fatalities per 100-million vehicle-miles traveled) as calculated and categorized by NHTSA as high-, mid-, and low-range states. We also factored in different types of programs (judiciary, administrative, and hybrid); states with low DWI fatalities or rates; and states with rural areas and tribal authorities, in selecting our state sample.

Although the information gathered from these 10 states are nongeneralizable, it provided insights about the extent of NHTSA's ignition interlock-related assistance, including its implementation of MAP-21 ignition-interlock grant program, and the ignition interlock-related research that states had conducted or participated in. In each state, we obtained information about the state's ignition interlock laws and program as well as any challenges in applying or qualifying for the MAP-21 ignition-interlock grant program. We also asked state officials about NHTSA's other ignition-interlock related assistance.

We conducted this performance audit from July 2013 to June 2014 in accordance with generally accepted government auditing standards, Those standards require that we plan and perform the audit to obtain sufficient, appropriate evidence to provide a reasonable basis for our findings and conclusions based on our audit objectives. We believe that the evidence obtained provides a reasonable basis for our findings and conclusions based on our audit objectives.

Appendix II: Studies on Ignition-Interlock Effectiveness

Beck, Kenneth H., William J. Rauch, Elizabeth A. Baker, and Alian F. Williams. "Effects of Ignition Interlock License Restrictions on Drivers With Multiple Alcohol Offenses: A Randomized Trial in Maryland." *American Journal of Public Health* 89(11) (1999): 1696-1700.

Bjerre, Bo. "Primary and secondary prevention of drinking and driving by the use of Alcolock device and program: the Swedish experience," in *Alcohol Ignition Interlock Devices, Volume II: Research, Policy, and Program Status* 2005. ed. Paul Marques (Oosterhout, Netherlands: International Council on Alcohol, Drugs and Traffic Safety (ICADTS), 2005), 11-24.

Coben, Jeffrey H., and Gregory L. Larkin. "Effectiveness of Ignition Interlock Devices in Reducing Drunk Driving Recidivism." *American Journal of Preventive Medicine*, 16(1S) (1999): 81-87.

DeYoung, David J., Helen N. Tashima, and Scott V. Masten. "An Evaluation of the Effectiveness of Ignition Interlock in California" in *Alcohol Ignition Interlock Devices – Volume II: Research, policy, and Program Status 2005*. ed. Paul Marques (Oosterhout, Netherlands: International Council on Alcohol, Drugs and Traffic Safety (ICADTS), 2005), 42-52.

Elder, Randy W., Robert Voas, Doug Beirness, Ruth A. Shults, David A. Sleet, James L. Nichols, and Richard Compton, Task Force on Community Preventive Services. "Effectiveness of Ignition Interlocks for Preventing Alcohol-Impaired Driving and Alcohol-Related Crashes. A Community Guide Systematic Review." *American Journal of Preventative Medicine* 40(3) (2011): 362-376.

EMT Group. "Evaluation of the California ignition interlock pilot program for DUI offenders." A report prepared for The California Department of Alcohol and Drug Programs and The California Office of Traffic Safety, 1990.

Jones, Barnie. "The Effectiveness of Oregon's Ignition-interlock program." Paper presented at the 12th International Conference on Alcohol, Drugs, and Traffic Safety, Cologne, Germany, September 28-October 2, 1992.

Marine, William. "High-tech solutions to drinking and driving: evaluation of a statewide, voluntary alcohol ignition-interlock program." Final grant report. University of Colorado Health Sciences Center (2001).

Marques, Paul R., A. Scott Tippetts, and Robert B. Voas. "Comparative and joint prediction of DUI recidivism from alcohol ignition interlock and driver records." *Journal of Studies on Alcohol*, 64(1) (2003): 83-92.

Marques, Paul R., Robert B. Voas, Richard Roth, and A. Scott Tippetts. *Evaluation of the New Mexico Ignition-interlock program.* A report prepared at the request of the National Highway Traffic Safety Administration, 2010.

Marques, Paul R., A. Scott Tippetts, and Robert B. Voas. "The Alcohol Interlock: An Underutilized Resource for Predicting and Controlling Drunk Drivers." *Traffic Injury Prevention*, 4:S1 (2006): 5-11.

Morse, Barbara J. and Delbert S. Elliott. "Effects of Ignition Interlock Devices on DUI Recidivism: Findings From a Longitudinal Study in Hamilton County, Ohio." *Crime & Delinquency* 38 (2) (1992): 131-157.

Popkin, Carol Lederhaus, J. Richard Stewart, Jo Beckmeyer, and Carol Martell. "An evaluation of the effectiveness of interlock systems in preventing DWI recidivism among second-time DWI offenders." Paper presented at the 12th International Conference on Alcohol, Drugs, and Traffic Safety, Cologne, Germany, September 28-October 2, 1992.

Raub, Richard A., Rov E. Lucke, and Richard Wark. "Breath alcohol ignition interlock devices: controlling the recidivist." *Traffic Injury Prevention* 4 (2003):199 –205.

Rauch, William J., Eileen M. Ahlin, Paul L. Zador, Jan M. Howard, and G. Doug Duncan. "Effects of administrative ignition interlock license restrictions on drivers with multiple alcohol offenses." Journal of Experimental Criminology 7 (2011): 127-148.

Roth, Richard, Robert Voas, and Paul Marques. "Mandating Interlocks for Fully Revoked Offenders: The New Mexico Experience." *Traffic Injury Prevention*, 8 (2007): 20-25.

Tippetts, A. Scott, and Robert B. Voas. "The effectiveness of the West Virginia interlock program." *Journal of Traffic Medicine* 26 (1998):19-24.

Vanlaar, Ward, Anna McKiernan, and Robyn Robertson. "Behavioral Patterns of Interlocked Offenders: Phase II." *Traffic Injury Research Foundation* (2013).

Vanlaar, Ward, Robyn Robertson, Desirée Schaap, and Jan Vissers. "Understanding Behavioural Patterns of Interlocked Offenders to Inform the Efficient and Effective Implementation of Interlock Programs: How Offenders on an Interlock Learn to Comply." *Traffic Injury Research Foundation* (2010).

Vezina, L. "The Quebec alcohol ignition-interlock program: impact on recidivism and crashes." Proceedings of the 16th International Conference on Alcohol, Drugs and Traffic Safety, Montreal, Canada, August 4-9, 2002.

Voas, Robert B., Anthony S. Tippetts, and Milton Grosz. "Administrative Reinstatement Interlock Programs: Florida, A 10-Year Study." *Alcoholism: Clinical and Experimental Research* 37(7) (2013): 1243-1251.

Voas, Robert B., Kenneth O. Blackman, A. Scott Tippetts, and Paul R. Marques. "Evaluation of a program to motivate impaired driving offenders to install ignition interlocks." *Accident Analysis and Prevention* 34 (2002): 449-455.

Voas, Robert B., Paul R. Marques, A. Scott Tippetts, and Douglas J. Beirness. "The Alberta interlock program: The evaluation of a province-wide program on DUI recidivism." *Addiction* 94(12) (1999): 1849-1859.

Willis, C., S. Lybrand, and N. Bellamy. "Alcohol ignition-interlock programmes for reducing drink driving recidivism (Review). *The Cochrane Database of Systematic Reviews* (2004): 1-20.

Zador, Paul L., Eileen M. Ahlin, William J. Rauch, Jan M. Howard, and G. Doug Duncan. "The effects of closer monitoring on driver compliance with interlock restrictions." *Accident Analysis and Prevention* 43 (2011): 1960-1967.

Appendix III: GAO Contact and Staff Acknowledgments

GAO Contact	Susan A. Fleming, (202) 512-2834 or Flemings@gao.gov
Staff Acknowledgments	In addition to the contact above, Sara Vermillion (Assistant Director); Melissa Bodeau; Russell Burnett; Leia Dickerson; Sarah Farkas; Geoffrey Hamilton; Kirsten Lauber; Gail Marnik; Josh Ormond; Friendly Vang-Johnson; and Elizabeth Wood made key contributions to this report.

www.ingramcontent.com/pod-product-compliance
Lightning Source LLC
Chambersburg PA
CBHW080638290526
45790CB00007B/3123